I0410125

Mastering Your Money

13 Clear And Concise Tips To Guide You To Financial Freedom

J Cleveland Payne

Copyright © 2023 J Cleveland Payne

All rights reserved.

ISBN: 9798862124279

Dedication

This book is dedicated to everyone with a strong idea of the accomplishments they want to achieve and waits for the right time to act while always working hard to ensure that time comes. You will be ready.

Keep your powder dry and keep your eye on the target. That opportunity is coming.

Table of Contents

Introduction: Why These 13 Tips To Master?

I have been writing about personal development in some shape or fashion for about 30 years.

While I have spent a good part of the last 20 years defining my personal development work as teaching others about working on oneself, I have never delved very deep into one's personal finances as a part of that work.

I manage two small businesses personally: a business consultant and a media creator. I know how to set a budget and manage resources from my many years in Acquisitions, Project Management, and Operations.

So, I know how to manage million-dollar account budgets. I know how to teach budget management from the perspective of a corporation or government agency. But to give you a moment of pure honesty, I could use serious improvement to manage my finances.

I spent about nine months early in my Air Force career as the living embodiment of the checkbook for a program where I produced a 2 million dollar contract for printers on my first day, a little under $150 million by the time I handed over my keys to head off my duty stations. And I still had to be counseled twice in that timeframe for not correctly turning in my travel expense reports.

Over time, I have reviewed many different personal finance programs and worked with various personal finance apps. I wish it were purely for research for other projects, but I was trying to find a simple way to manage my own money and a way to turn it into minimum effort.

I can navigate complex financial spreadsheets and multi-year contract requirements. Still, since the need to balance physical checkbooks was done away with the mass adoption of debit cards and online banking, I was always at a loss of just how much walking around money I could pull without incurring the wrath of an overdraft charge.

So why am I writing a book on personal finance? I learn best by doing research, so this is party a batch of lessons for myself that I am sharing with the class since I did all this work (not the time to complain about being stuck with all the work from group projects past, but...).

Part of the motivation, honesty, is brand building. As I stated earlier, I manage a business consultancy where I guide small business owners and side hustlers on how to keep their professional houses in order with processes and practices. Keeping your petty cash away from your pocket change goes a long way to increasing the odds of continued business success.

Bonus for me is that at the time of this writing, I am playing catch up on the amount of written content I was unable to produce during the pandemic years as I ironically put my creative focus into learning how to create more video content and was sidetrack by a lot of emergencies at the day job.

Why produce a traditionally unlucky number of 13 tips to present? Did the title get your attention? Mission Accomplished!

Those 13 tips detailed in this book are simple concepts to grasp, even if the execution requires more mental effort and real-world willpower than you may be willing to give currently.

They are: set clear financial goals, create a budget, build an emergency fund, reduce debt, save consistently, invest wisely, monitor your credit score, live below your means, continuously educate yourself, avoid unnecessary fees, practice regular financial reviews, ensure proper insurance, and plan for taxes.

Each chapter covers one of the 13 tips in greater detail, breaking the topic down into five distinct principles to help you understand why they are essential to giving you actual instructions on how to finally incorporate each tip into your life.

This book is a rare do as I am doing with you journey to better personal financial health. Writing (and living the principles) of this book has been a long time coming for me, but I am truly ready to take this journey and get to the other side of working through all the tips. I am glad this book found its way into your hands

and happy to have you taking the journey
alongside me.

Chapter 1: Set Clear Financial Goals

Navigating the world of personal finance might sometimes feel like trying to sail through uncharted waters. However, just as every sailor needs a compass, every individual aiming for financial success needs to set clear financial goals. Imagine yourself setting sail with no destination in mind. You'd quickly find yourself adrift, wouldn't you? In the same manner, without financial goals, you'd be aimlessly spending and saving, which isn't the most efficient way to achieve financial health.

Let's launch this journey together by properly charting a course to financial stability.

1. Define Short-Term Goals

We all have those immediate wishes, those things that make us say, "I'd like to do/have this by the end of the year!" These are our short-term goals. These are easy to see and relatively easy to achieve. They can be the simple boosts to help you achieve other goals not so easy to see from where you are currently standing.

The Characteristics of Short-Term Goals:

- They usually span from a month to a year.
- They are precise and quantifiable. Instead of saying, "I want to save money," you might say, "I want to save $500 for a new laptop."
- They are often stepping stones towards medium or long-term goals.

Tips to Define Them:

- Write them down! Use a journal, a mobile app, or sticky notes on your fridge.
- Make them S.M.A.R.T: Specific, Measurable, Achievable, Relevant, Time-bound.
- Celebrate once you achieve them. It will fuel your motivation for bigger challenges.

2. Establish Medium-Term Goals

While short-term goals are easy to get to and check off a list. Medium-term goals represent the bigger wants with more intricate needs. They might not be right around the corner, but they're achievable with more dedication.

What Qualifies as a Medium-Term Goal?

- These typically span over one to five years.
- They might be more complex, like saving for a down payment on a home, starting a business, or funding a higher education course.
- Often, they require a more structured financial plan.

Establishing These Goals:

- Research and get a clear estimate of the financial implication. If it's a car, how much does your desired model cost?
- Consider inflation. The cost of a product or service might rise over time.
- Automate savings. If you're saving for that car, consider setting up a separate account and automating transfers to it.

3. Visualize Long-Term Goals

You are still responsible for that goal too far in the distance to keep in your crosshairs daily.

Your long-term goals are the dreams you wish to achieve way down the line. They are your ultimate financial destination.

Understanding Long-Term Goals:

- They extend beyond five years and might even stretch up to retirement.
- They can be complex, like achieving a certain net worth, fully paying off a mortgage, or ensuring a comfortable retirement.
- Long-term goals often require investments, not just savings.

How to Visualize Them:

- Dream big, but be realistic. While it's good to aim for the stars, grounding your goals in reality helps make them achievable.
- Consult with financial advisors. They can offer expert guidance on how to invest and grow your wealth.
- Be patient. These goals take time. Remember, the bigger the tree, the deeper the roots.

4. Prioritize Your Goals

Imagine having a map filled with sites and destinations you'd like to visit but without a clear path. Prioritizing your goals ensures that you're not stretching yourself too thin and focusing on what matters most.

Steps to Prioritize:

- List all your goals: short, medium, and long-term.
- Analyze their urgency and importance. Paying off high-interest debt might come before saving for a vacation.
- Consider dependencies. Sometimes, one goal leads to another. For instance, securing a stable job (short-term) might be a precursor to buying a home (medium-term).
- Flexibility is key. Life is unpredictable. Adjust your priorities, when necessary, but keep the bigger picture in mind.

5. Review Regularly

Setting goals isn't a "set and forget" kind of deal. In naval navigation, a captain must regularly check the ship's compass. You must do the same with regular reviews of your financial goals.

Why Reviews are Essential:

- They help you stay on track.
- Life changes: marriage, kids, new jobs, or unexpected expenses can change your financial landscape.
- The financial market evolves. Investment opportunities from five years ago might not be relevant today.

Reviewing Done Right:

- Set aside time. Whether it's quarterly, bi-annually, or annually, ensure you have a dedicated time to review your goals.
- Re-evaluate and adjust. Perhaps you've earned a raise (congratulations!), and you can now allocate more towards your goals.
- Celebrate your milestones, no matter how small. Every achievement is a step closer to your ultimate financial dream.

Clear financial goals are your North Star to help you maintain your bearings as you work to improve your personal finances. By defining short, medium, and long-term goals, prioritizing them, and conducting regular reviews, you ensure you have a course to follow and don't drift too far off. Better personal financial management does not happen by just filing a plan and waiting for it to work itself out operations. You (and I) have a long way to go: 12 more chapters plus a lot of trial and error to see how well it works lies ahead.

14

Chapter 2: Create a Budget

One tip revealed towards the goal of being better at our personal finances, and that first tip was getting clear with what the end goal should look like when you get there. This chapter is about taking that target goal and working with an essential tool to help you eventually achieve it. No magic bullets are offered here, and there is a long way to go, but it all starts with more personal information put down on paper: budgeting.

And this starts with the question everyone asks as a pushback, "Why do I need a budget?" Imagine going on a cross-country road trip without a roadmap. You can call getting lost an easy prediction. You won't know how far away you are from anything, so you will spend extra time trying to find your bearings and likely run out of fuel on multiple occasions. A budget acts as more than a simple map. It guides you to reach your financial destinations efficiently and with fewer detours.

Let's begin the work to craft a budget perfect for your needs.

1. List Your Income Sources

Before you determine how to allocate your money, you need to know how much money you're working with.

What Counts as Income?

- Primary Income: This is the wage or salary you earn from your job.
- Secondary Income: Do you freelance? Maybe you rent out a room on Airbnb. These count, too!
- Passive Income: Royalties, dividends, or perhaps revenue from a blog.
- One-Time Incomes: Bonuses, gifts, or perhaps the sale of an item.

Mapping Your Income:

- Document all consistent sources.
- Add any occasional or one-time incomes but differentiate them, as they aren't regular.
- If your income varies (as it might for freelancers), consider taking an average of the past six months or projecting a conservative estimate.

2. Itemize Monthly Expenses

We've taken time to identify all your income, hopefully in great detail. Now, it's time to account for all the cash you are sending out, in manners valid and not, which is the absolute bane of your money woes.

Common Monthly Expenses:

- Fixed Costs: These remain consistent. Think rent, mortgage, or insurance.
- Variable Costs: Groceries, utility bills, dining out – they can fluctuate.
- Non-Monthly Expenses: Annual fees or quarterly bills? Divide them by 12 to get a monthly amount.

Itemizing like a Pro:

- Keep receipts or check bank statements to track where your money goes.
- Use budgeting apps or good old-fashioned spreadsheets.
- Remember, no expense is too small. That daily coffee can add up over a month!

3. Categorize Spending

With expenses listed, it's time to organize them. Much like sorting your laundry, you'll need different "baskets" for different spending types.

Popular Spending Categories:

- Essentials: Housing, food, utilities, and transportation.
- Financial Goals: Savings, investments, and debt repayments.
- Non-Essentials: Dining out, hobbies, entertainment, and vacations.

Categorizing Efficiently:

- Personalize categories based on your lifestyle. Maybe you're a student and need a "textbooks" category.
- Avoid too many categories. While you should be detailed, having 50 categories can be overwhelming. Find a balance.
- Re-evaluate periodically. As your life changes, your categories might too.

4. Set Spending Limits

It's time for you to take some control of your financial life. Allocating specific amounts to each category ensures you have enough fuel to successfully reach your financial journey's end.

Setting Realistic Limits:

- Base them on past spending. If you've historically spent $200 on groceries, setting a $100 limit might be unrealistic.
- Consider your financial goals. If you aim to save more, perhaps cut back on non-essential spending.
- Remember, it's not about cutting joy out of your life. It's about making sure your spending aligns with your values and goals.

5. Track and Adjust

Setting your budget isn't the end. It's a living, breathing entity that needs check-ups and adjustments.

The Importance of Tracking:

- Helps identify bad spending habits.
- Ensures you're on course to hit your financial goals.
- Allows you to anticipate and prepare for larger expenses.

How to Adjust:

- If you consistently overspend in a category, revisit it. Maybe the limit was unrealistic, or perhaps you need to rein in spending.
- Unexpected income? Great! Decide where it can best be used – perhaps accelerating a financial goal or treating yourself.
- Periodic reviews, such as monthly or quarterly, are ideal.

It is important to remember this when creating a budget: this isn't a punishment or restriction. It is your liberation from the burden of never knowing where your money is supposed to be. This metaphorical roadmap ensures you spend with intention, aligning your resources with your values and dreams. As with any map, sometimes you'll have no choice but to take detours to get to the planned destination eventually. And that is okay. Regular check-ins and adjustments will help you return to the predictable path.

For now, give yourself a pat on the back for working through the budgeting process. This step is a huge one towards financial mastery.

Chapter 3: Build an Emergency Fund

The third tip I'm presenting on improving your finances will probably be hard. We're going into deep detail about ensuring a safety net to turn to in times of need. The Emergency Fund (in all caps as a proper noun to show just how big a thing it is) functions as the lifeboat of your financial ship. This metaphor should continue to resonate as the imagery raises the drama of the situation: being stuck in a crisis with no visible way out.

Don't get overly stressed by believing you must rob a bank today to ensure you have this fund set for tomorrow. Let's start the process of building this indispensable fund:

1. Determine Fund Size

First things first, how large should this fund be? Every person's situation varies. The size and structure of a fund must depend on every individual and their unique financial circumstances. You must start with an honest look at yourself and your unique situation.

Understanding Your Needs:

- Most experts recommend having enough to cover three to six months' worth of essential expenses. This includes your rent or mortgage, utility bills, groceries, and any regular debt payments.
- However, if your job is freelance-based or commission-based (meaning your income is irregular), consider a larger safety net, perhaps extending to 9-12 months of expenses.
- Factor in dependents. If you have children or other family members relying on your income, a heftier fund can bring added peace of mind.

2. Start Small

I am sure you have heard the phrase, "Every journey starts with a single step." If saving up several months' worth of expenses feels daunting, fret not. Begin with what you can. It's the build-up from that first ten dollars you get from skipping one lunch or that first leap of faith with a direct deposit from your paycheck. It's not about how much you save immediately but about building the habit of saving.

Baby Steps to Success:

- Start with a goal that feels achievable, perhaps $500 or $1,000.
- Each time you reach a milestone, celebrate it! Then, set your sights on a new target.
- Consider using windfalls. Tax refunds, bonuses, or any unexpected inflow can be an excellent booster for your emergency fund.

3. Choose Accessible Accounts

Your emergency fund should be like the lifeboat hanging on the side of a ship—ready to be launched at a moment's notice. This isn't the money you want tied up in intricate investments.

Choosing the Right Home for Your Fund:

- Savings Accounts are a classic choice. They are liquid, meaning you can withdraw funds whenever necessary. Many even offer decent interest rates.
- Money Market Accounts can sometimes provide higher interest rates than standard savings accounts, but they may come with minimum balance requirements.

- Stay away from high-risk investments for this money. The idea is safety and accessibility over high returns.
- Make sure the account you choose doesn't penalize you for withdrawals, as this defeats the purpose of an emergency fund.

4. Avoid Touching It

The temptation to spend your savings as you watch it grow will be enormous! When you see that money sitting there, using it for a spontaneous vacation or the latest tech gadget can be alluring. But remember: the "emergency" in "emergency fund" is reserved for genuine emergencies only.

When to Use the Fund:

- True Emergencies like medical emergencies, unexpected car repairs, sudden home repairs, or unforeseen job loss.
- Avoid Using For Planned Expenses: Vacations, holidays, and expected bills aren't emergencies.
- Before tapping into the fund, ask yourself, "Is this a want or a need?"

- If you do use the money, prioritize replenishing it. You never know when another emergency might arise.

5. Review and Adjust

Like all aspects of personal finance, your emergency fund isn't a static entity. As life evolves, so should your safety net.

Adapting to Life's Changes:

- Change in Household Size: A new baby, a family member moving in, or even a pet can change monthly expenses.
- Shifts in Income: A significant raise, or on the flip side, a decrease in household income, should prompt a re-evaluation.
- Major Life Events: Purchasing a home, changes in marital status, or even shifting to a more volatile job sector can all impact the size of the fund you need.
- Make it a habit to review your emergency fund at least annually or after any major financial change.

Building and maintaining an emergency fund might not be the most glamorous part of personal finance, but it's one of the most crucial. This fund can keep you stable, with no need to panic when you encounter a financial catastrophe. It takes time to build, and you may need more funds ready for an upcoming emergency that will almost certainly happen.

Keeping with the sailing metaphor, all you can do is stay the course. This fund will grow to a sizable amount with less energy than you think if you keep focused on the purpose: to ensure peace of mind when the storm does roll into your world.

Chapter 4: Reduce Debt

Greetings to you, dear reader, as we approach the mountainous terrain of debt in our journey through personal finance. If you've ever felt the weight of debt bearing down on you, you're not alone. Many find themselves in a whirlpool of borrowings, not knowing how to navigate their way out. However, every mountain can be scaled, and every whirlpool can be escaped—with the right strategy. Let's embark on this voyage to reduce and eventually free ourselves from the chains of debt.

1. Prioritize High-Interest Debt

Imagine being chased by a pack of wolves. Some are faster than others. The high-interest debts? They're the quickest wolves nipping at your heels.

Understanding High-Interest Debt:

- They grow rapidly. A credit card debt might seem small, but with high interest, it can snowball quickly.
- The longer you take to clear them, the more you end up paying.

- Common culprits include credit cards, payday loans, and certain personal loans.

Taking Action:

- List down all your debts, noting their interest rates.
- Allocate extra funds towards these high-interest debts first. It's called the 'avalanche method,' which aims to minimize the amount paid over time.
- Keep paying the minimum amounts on other loans to avoid fees and penalties.

2. Avoid New Debt

Our goal is to escape the whirlpool, not dive deeper. While it's tempting to swipe that credit card or take another loan, it's essential to exercise restraint.

The Traps of New Debt:

- Every new debt adds to your monthly obligations.
- It can push back other financial goals, like saving or investing.

- Mental well-being can be affected, as increased debt can lead to increased stress.

How to Steer Clear:

- Limit credit card usage to what you can pay off in full each month.
- Before taking new debt, ask yourself if it's absolutely necessary. Can it wait?
- Build an emergency fund. It's your shield against unforeseen expenses, reducing the need to borrow.

3. Set Debt Reduction Goals

Sailing without a destination can have you adrift indefinitely. Similarly, without clear goals, debt reduction can seem like an endless journey.

The Power of Setting Goals:

- It provides direction, ensuring you're moving forward, not in circles.
- Clear goals can be motivating. Seeing a target number drop month after month can be exhilarating.

- It allows for structured planning.

Mapping Out Your Goals:

- Break down your total debt into smaller, more manageable targets.
- Determine a timeline. Decide by when you'd like to be debt-free or have a certain debt cleared.
- Monitor progress. Keeping tabs helps in adjusting your strategy if needed.

4. Negotiate Interest Rates

You might wonder, "Can I really do that?" Yes, you can! While it's not guaranteed, with a little courage and the right approach, you can negotiate your way to lower interest rates.

Why Negotiate:

- Even a small percentage drop can result in significant savings over time.
- Lenders might be willing to accommodate if they believe there's a risk of default or if you've been a long-

standing customer with a good track record.

- Lower rates can accelerate your debt clearance.

The Art of Negotiation:

- Do your homework. Know prevailing interest rates and where you stand.
- Be polite yet assertive. Explain your situation and why you believe a rate reduction is fair.
- If one lender doesn't budge, consider transferring balances or consolidating debts where lower rates are offered.

5. Celebrate Small Wins

It's a marathon, not a sprint. And every mile conquered deserves its own cheer.

The Importance of Celebrating:

- It keeps morale high. Debt reduction can be a long and sometimes disheartening journey.

- Celebrations act as reminders of progress made.
- Small wins pave the path to big victories.

Ideas for Celebration:

- Did you clear that pesky credit card debt? Treat yourself to a movie or a modest dinner out.
- Create a visual tracker. Color in segments as you knock out portions of your debt—it's satisfying!
- Share your progress with a supportive friend or family member. Sometimes, just talking about it feels rewarding.

In conclusion, while the shadows of debt might seem long and daunting, with the right strategy and mindset, they can be overcome. Prioritizing high-interest debts, avoiding new ones, setting clear goals, negotiating rates, and celebrating small wins are your tools in this mission. Remember, every great journey begins with the decision to take the first step. And with each step, you're closer to financial freedom. Here's to conquering that debt mountain!

Chapter 5: Save Consistently

If financial stability were a structure, consistent savings would be its foundation. Think of it as a reservoir; you don't just fill it up once and forget about it. Instead, you continuously divert a stream to it, ensuring its level remains stable even if you occasionally tap into it. Consistent saving is about creating a solid financial safety net, so when unexpected expenses come raining down, you have an umbrella of savings to keep you dry.

Let's dive into how you can turn saving from an occasional thought into a consistent habit.

1. Set Automatic Transfers

In a world of automation, why should our savings lag behind?

The Magic of Automation:

- Set it and (almost) forget it: Once set, automatic transfers ensure a part of your income goes straight into savings without you having to lift a finger.
- Out of sight, out of mind: By automating, you prevent the temptation to spend

money that's sitting in your main account. Before you even see it, it's already nestled safely in savings.

Setting Automatic Transfers:

- Choose a date, ideally just after your paycheck clears, so your account is flush.
- Decide on a fixed amount or percentage of your income to divert.
- Review your main account regularly to ensure there's no hiccups with the transfers.

2. Choose Right Savings Vehicle

Not all savings are created equal. Think of it this way: would you store your precious photo albums (remember those?) in a damp basement? Of course not! Similarly, choose the right place for your savings.

Types of Savings Vehicles:

- Savings Account: Easily accessible and best for short-term goals or emergency funds.

- Fixed Deposits or CDs: Locks your money for a predetermined period, often at higher interest rates than regular savings accounts.
- Money Market Accounts: Typically earns more interest than a savings account but might require a higher minimum balance.
- Retirement Accounts (like 401(k), IRAs): These are long-term, often with tax advantages but with restrictions on withdrawal.

How to Choose:

- Assess your goals. Need money in the short term? Go for a savings account. Thinking of retirement? Look into retirement accounts.
- Compare interest rates.
- Understand terms and conditions, especially any restrictions on accessing your money.

3. Adjust As Income Changes

You will need to make adjustments as changes to your income occur over time. Whether you claim that long-standing promotion or suffer a temporary layoff, you need to understand how to adjust your savings with your income.

Why Adjustments Matter:

- Increased Income: If you've received a raise or taken on additional work, consider ramping up your savings. More money can often lead to more spending unless you channel it wisely.
- Decreased Income: Tough times might require a momentary reduction in savings. It's okay. Prioritize essentials, but aim to get back on track as soon as possible.

How to Make Adjustments:

- Review your budget whenever there's a significant change in income.
- If increasing savings, decide where the extra should go: perhaps split between short-term savings and long-term investments.
- Stay informed on your needs. Perhaps earlier, you were single and now you have a family to consider. Adjust savings accordingly.

4. Diversify Savings

As the saying goes, never put all your eggs—or in this case, dollars—in one basket.

Why Diversification is Crucial:

- Different savings vehicles offer different benefits.
- Economic fluctuations can affect interest rates. Diversifying safeguards you from potential downturns in one area.

Ways to Diversify:

- Split savings between liquid accounts (like regular savings) and more fixed options (like CDs or bonds).
- Consider a mix of risk. While savings accounts are low risk, you might consider investing a portion in stocks for potentially higher returns.
- Continuously educate yourself. The financial landscape is ever-evolving. What's relevant today might be outdated tomorrow.

5. Stay Disciplined

Consistency is born out of discipline. Just as a fitness routine yields results only with regularity, so does saving.

Why Discipline Matters:

- It's easy to be swayed by market trends or personal desires.
- Emergencies aren't scheduled. Having a consistent saving habit ensures you're always prepared.

Staying on the Path:

- Remember your financial goals. Visualize them. Perhaps even create a vision board.
- Reward yourself occasionally, but not from your savings! Allocate a separate treat fund.
- Surround yourself with like-minded savers. Sharing experiences can be both educational and motivating.

Remember, consistent saving is not a punishment. It is not about depriving yourself but ensuring you're always prepared. It is all about building a future where you're in total control of your money. A penny saved might be a penny earned, but a penny saved consistently? That's the cornerstone of a prosperous financial future. So, gear up, set those transfers, and let's build that reservoir, one drop (or dollar) at a time!

Chapter 6: Invest Wisely

So, you've set good financial goals, are budgeting like a pro, and are now looking to jump into the rewarding (yet sometimes unpredictable) world of investments. This chapter, aptly titled 'Invest Wisely,' is your trusty guide to do just that.

Investing isn't just about stashing money somewhere and hoping for the best. It's about making your money work for you, strategically and judiciously. Let's delve into five essential signposts to guide you.

1. Educate Yourself

The Investment World is vast:
Choice can be a detriment in life. Having more options leads to choice paralysis. The world of investing offers a multitude of options: stocks, bonds, real estate, commodities, cryptocurrencies, and the list goes on. Tossing your money into any of these without understanding their fundamentals can lead to, let's say, some unexpected returns!

Steps to Becoming Investment-Savvy:

- Start with the Basics: Understand terms like dividends, capital gains, yield, and ROI. Think of them as the language of the investment world.
- Read Widely: From classics like "The Intelligent Investor" by Benjamin Graham to modern insights from blogs and websites, immerse yourself.
- Engage in Online Courses: Many platforms offer courses on investment basics. Why not turn your weekend into a learning fest?
- Join Forums: Engage with fellow investors. It's like joining a sailors' club, where shared experiences can be eye-opening.

2. Diversify Portfolio

Why All Eggs in One Basket isn't Wise:
Have you ever heard of the Titanic? It was an unsinkable ship, yet it was no match for an iceberg and sank after impact. If you put all your investment into one stock or type and it goes south, your entire portfolio might slip into the freezing water's depts!

The Beauty of Diversification:

- Spread Risks: Different investments come with varying levels of risks. By diversifying, you ensure not everything is affected by one sector's downturn.
- Potential for Better Returns: While one segment might be performing poorly, others might be thriving.
- Tip to Diversify: Aim for a mix of asset classes (stocks, bonds, real estate, etc.). Within each class, diversify further: different industries, regions, and risk levels.

3. Start Early

The Early Bird Catches the Worm:
Or, in our sea analogy, the early sailor catches the best winds! The sooner you start, the longer your money has to grow, thanks to the magic of compound interest.

Why Timing Matters:

- Power of Compound Interest: Imagine earning interest on your investment, and then in subsequent periods, earning interest on the initial sum and the previously earned interest. Over time, this snowballs!

- Weathering Storms: Starting early gives your investments more time to recover from market downturns.
- Financial Discipline: Starting young instills a habit, turning you into a disciplined investor.

4. Review Portfolio Periodically

Why Set Sail and Forget isn't the Best Strategy: As we lean heavily on the nautical metaphors in this chapter, think of the open sea as ever-changing. The same calm waters you may sail through today might be stormy tomorrow. Similarly, the financial markets are just as dynamic.

The Importance of Regular Check-ins:

- Performance Analysis: Maybe one segment of your portfolio has been outperforming, while another lags. Reviews help identify these trends.
- Rebalancing: Over time, due to different performances, your portfolio might drift from its original asset allocation. Periodic reviews help rebalance to your desired mix.

- Staying Updated: It keeps you informed about global events that might affect your investments. Think of it as checking the weather report before setting sail.

5. Consult Professionals

Why You Might Need a Navigator:
No matter how skilled, even the best sailors sometimes consult navigation experts. In the world of investing, these are your financial advisors.

Advantages of Professional Consultation:

- Expert Insights: They're abreast of market trends and can provide guidance tailored to your financial goals.
- Emotional Neutrality: It's easy to get emotionally attached to certain investments. Professionals provide an objective viewpoint.
- Planning for the Future: They can help in structuring your investments according to future needs, like retirement.

Choosing the Right Advisor:

- Credentials Matter: Look for certifications, like Certified Financial Planner (CFP) or Chartered Financial Analyst (CFA).
- Transparency: Ensure they're upfront about their fees.
- Seek Recommendations: Sometimes, the best advisors are found through word of mouth. Ask friends, family, or colleagues.

Investing is an adventure full of excitement and mystery. Seeing your money grow and anticipating market trends and strategies is thrilling—it's all part of the experience. And as with any expedition, the journey is smoother when you're well-prepared and informed. By educating yourself, diversifying your assets, starting early, keeping a vigilant eye, and occasionally seeking expert guidance, you're not just setting sail—you're charting a course to financial prosperity.

Chapter 7: Monitor Your Credit Score

As we delve deeper into the world of personal finance management, one point of consistently you will learn to love (or at least greatly respect and tolerate) is your credit score. Think of this score as a power source to drive you forward in your financial endeavors. You would like the ride to be as fast and smooth as possible. But to ensure all is well, you must regularly check this number in its many forms and understand the forces that can change it. This chapter will detail how to keep that credit score to your financial advantage.

1. Check Reports Annually

Imagine if your ship had a small, annoying, but manageable leak. Left unattended, it will soon lead to much more significant issues. Similarly, minor discrepancies in your credit report can snowball into more significant concerns.

Why Annual Checks Matter:

- Spotting Identity Theft: Early detection of any unauthorized credit applications can be a lifesaver.

- Catching Errors: Sometimes, credit bureaus or lenders make mistakes that might affect your score.
- Understanding Your Financial Health: Knowing where you stand can help you set goals.

How to Do It:

- Avail your free reports. In many regions, you're entitled to a free annual report from major credit bureaus.
- Set a reminder. Mark a specific date on your calendar, so you never miss out.

2. Understand Score Factors

Various factors influence your credit score. Getting as much knowledge as possible can empower you to maintain a higher score and enjoy the benefits that go along with it..

Key Factors Include:

- Payment History: Timely bill payments are paramount. They signify your reliability.

- Credit Utilization: This represents how much credit you're using against your total available limit. Lower utilization often leads to a higher score.
- Length of Credit History: Lenders like to see a longer track record of responsible credit use.
- Types of Credit: A mix, like credit cards, mortgages, and installment loans, can be favorable.
- Recent Inquiries: Every time you apply for credit, it can create a mark on your report.

What This Means for You:

- Timely payments and sensible credit use are cornerstones.
- If you're new to credit, even small positive actions can yield improvements.

3. Avoid Unnecessary Hard Inquiries

It is not bad to know your score, but one of the worst offenses that can affect your score directly is repeated inquiries, which happens every time a company wants to know you are worthy. Too many inquiries can be a red flag to single you out as a credit abuser.

Understanding Hard Inquiries:

- These are checks done by lenders or credit providers when you apply for credit.
- Each hard inquiry can slightly drop your score.
- They remain on your report for about two years, though the impact on your score diminishes over time.

How to Navigate Them:

- Only apply for credit when truly necessary.
- If shopping for a loan, do so within a short window (often 14-45 days, depending on the scoring model) so that multiple inquiries are treated as a single one for scoring purposes.

4. Settle Due Bills

Consider all your unsettled bills as extra weight strapped to your back for no reason, slowing down your progress. The weight might seem small initially, but it can drag you down over time.

The Impact of Unsettled Bills:

- Late payments can severely dent your score, especially if they become a pattern.
- They remain on your credit report for years and can signal to lenders that you're a risky borrower.

Charting a Course:

- Set reminders or automate bill payments to avoid missing due dates.
- If you anticipate difficulty in making a payment, contact the creditor. They might offer solutions or temporary leniency.

5. Report Inaccuracies

In the world of credit scores, inaccuracies in your report can misguide lenders and unjustly affect your score. Like a poorly copied map, you may not qualify for the credit considerations you deserve if the path needed to navigate your score needs to be corrected.

How Inaccuracies Occur:

- Clerical errors during data entry.
- Mix-ups due to common names or errors in addresses.
- Fraudulent activities or identity theft.

Correcting Your Map:

- Dispute any inaccuracies with the respective credit bureau. They are typically required to investigate (usually within 30 days).
- Be ready with documentation to support your dispute.
- Keep track of all communications and follow up until the error is rectified.

Maintaining a solid credit score is about more than just the credit you want access to today.

It's also about ensuring that when financial challenges and economic uncertainties arise, you're well-prepared to outlast them. Your best tools are regular (but not excessive) credit checks, understanding score dynamics, and timely interventions. Set your sights on attainable financial goals with a strong command of your credit score, and you will find yourself in a better position to enjoy the journey.

Chapter 8: Live Below Your Means

When anyone thoroughly reviews personal finance education, one mantra always stands out as a beacon of wisdom: "Live below your means." Before envisioning a life stripped of all joys, let's clarify: living below your means doesn't translate to forsaking all pleasure. Instead, it's about cultivating mindfulness, making intentional choices, and embracing a sense of abundance even within boundaries. Let's journey together through this enlightening concept.

1. Differentiate Wants vs. Needs

Before making any purchase, ask yourself this simple yet profound question: "Do I want this, or do I need this?" Understanding the distinction is pivotal.

Characteristics of Needs:

- Essential for Survival: Think food, shelter, and clothing. Without them, daily life becomes a challenge.
- Foundational: These are often recurring, like groceries, utilities, and transportation.

Characteristics of Wants:

- Desirable but Non-Essential: That fancy new gadget, the latest designer purse, or an extravagant vacation.
- Often Influenced by External Factors: Peer pressure, societal expectations, or flashy advertisements can nudge our desires.

Action Point: Before spending, pause and reflect. Will this purchase genuinely add value to your life, or is it a fleeting urge?

2. Adopt Minimalism

At its core, minimalism isn't about owning as few items as possible; it's about owning only what adds value to your life.

Why Embrace Minimalism?

- Clears Physical and Mental Clutter: Fewer items mean less to maintain, clean, and worry about.
- Boosts Financial Health: Owning fewer things often means spending less money.

- Fosters Appreciation: When you only have what truly matters, you begin to appreciate those items more.

Steps to Adopt Minimalism:

- Evaluate Possessions: Do they serve a purpose or bring joy?
- Buy Quality over Quantity: It might be more expensive initially, but quality items often last longer, proving cost-effective in the long run.
- Be Intentional: Before making a purchase, ask if it aligns with your minimalist ethos.

3. Avoid Impulse Purchases

Spontaneous shopping sprees! Exhilarating, exciting, and often leading to long bouts of buyer's remorse. Here's why and how to resist.

Understand the Trigger:

- Emotional Shopping: Feeling low? Retail therapy is a common but ineffective bandage.

- The 'Sale' Trap: Just because it's discounted doesn't mean it's a good buy. If you weren't considering it at full price, do you truly need it?
- The Power of Advertising: Brands invest heavily in making their products irresistible.

Combatting Impulse Buying:

- The 24-Hour Rule: Wait 24 hours before buying. If you still want it after reflecting, then consider.
- Shop with a List: And stick to it! This especially helps in places like grocery stores.

4. Review Regular Expenses

Like a water bottle with a leak you can't see, unnoticed regular expenses can drain financial health right before your eyes. Periodic reviews can be a lifesaver.

Common Overlooked Expenses:

- Subscriptions: That magazine you no longer read or the app you rarely use.
- Upgraded Services: Are you using all the channels in your premium cable package? Could a smaller data plan work for your phone?

Reviewing Effectively:

- Dedicate Time: Perhaps once every quarter, sit down to review your bank and credit card statements.
- Ask the Tough Questions: Are you getting value from this expense? Could there be a cheaper alternative? Would eliminating it significantly affect your life quality?

5. Practice Delayed Gratification

In an age of instant everything – from downloads to deliveries – waiting seems old-fashioned. But embracing delayed gratification can lead to profound financial and personal growth.

Benefits:

- Reduced Buyer's Remorse: Waiting ensures you genuinely want and value the item.
- Improved Financial Position: Saving for a goal can lead to better deals (like buying with cash and avoiding interest) and less financial stress.

Building the Muscle of Patience:

- Visualize the End Goal: Whether it's a dream vacation or a new home, keep the bigger picture in mind.
- Create a Savings Goal: Track your progress. Celebrate milestones.
- Enjoy the Journey: Find joy in the anticipation, the research, and the buildup. Often, they're as fulfilling as the end goal.

Again, living below your means isn't about deprivation but liberation. It's about making choices that echo your values, prioritizing lasting joy over fleeting pleasure, and building a secure financial future. Right now is the perfect time for reflection on your spending habits. What changes can you embrace to live more abundantly yet below your means? Working toward financial mindfulness is a bold decision. Living below your means is a way to maintain that journey with little problem.

Chapter 9: Continuously Educate Yourself

Picture yourself walking through a large, lush forest with only a map that is becoming increasingly more outdated the longer you look at it. This map is akin to our existing knowledge in the ever-evolving landscape of personal finance. If we continuously update our knowledge, we'll likely retain our way. You are now tasked with moving deeper into this forest of financial wisdom, and the key is to remember one fundamental truth: knowledge is power. We will walk this path together and work to understand why continuous education is crucial and how to stay up-to-date.

1. Read Financial Books

Opening a book is like opening a door to a new world, one brimming with knowledge and insights.

The Magic of Financial Books:

- Depth of Content: Unlike articles or blogs, books usually provide a deeper dive into subjects. From understanding

stocks to mastering the art of budgeting, there's a book for every topic.
- Variety of Perspectives: Every author brings a unique perspective, enabling you to see an issue from multiple angles.
- Portable Wisdom: The convenience of carrying a book or having an e-book means you can imbibe knowledge anytime, anywhere.

Making the Most of It:

- Start with Classics: Titles like "Rich Dad Poor Dad" or "The Intelligent Investor" have stood the test of time for a reason.
- Diversify Your Reading: Don't just stick to one sub-topic. Delve into real estate, stocks, behavioral finance, and more.
- Discuss & Debate: Share what you've learned with friends or family. Discussing concepts can solidify your understanding.

2. Attend Workshops

Attending a workshop is a bit like attending a live concert. You experience the energy, interact directly with experts, and immerse yourself in the learning environment.

Why Workshops Work:

- Hands-on Learning: Many workshops offer practical exercises, allowing you to implement what you learn immediately.
- Networking Opportunities: Mingle with fellow attendees. Their experiences and insights could prove invaluable.
- Direct Interaction: Get your pressing questions answered right away by the experts.

How to Optimize the Experience:

- Be Prepared: Know the agenda and, if possible, read up a little. This ensures you can make the most of the interaction.
- Engage Actively: Participate in discussions, ask questions, and share your experiences.
- Post-Workshop Review: Take some time after the workshop to review and assimilate all you've learned.

3. Subscribe to Financial Blogs

In the digital age, learning has never been so accessible. Financial blogs are the modern-day newspapers of the finance world, providing current updates, trends, and insights.

The Beauty of Blogs:

- Up-to-Date: Financial landscapes change. Blogs offer real-time insights and analysis on recent developments.
- Diverse Voices: From seasoned experts to passionate amateurs, you get a spectrum of viewpoints.
- Bite-Sized Learning: Short on time? Blogs can be a quick read, perfect for those busy days.

Making Blogs Work for You:

- Curate Your List: Find bloggers whose style and expertise resonate with you.
- Engage: Comment on posts, ask questions, and participate in discussions. Many bloggers appreciate the interaction.
- Apply the Knowledge: If a particular tip or advice strikes a chord, try implementing it.

4. Join Financial Groups

You take a break from your trek through the metaphorical forest of learning financial principles because you're tired. It's hard work. In your imagination, you find a group sitting around a campfire, exchanging stories. Financial groups—whether online forums, community groups, or formal associations—are the campfires of our financial journey.

Why Groups Matter:

- Shared Experience: Learn from others' successes and mistakes. Real-life experiences often provide the best lessons.
- Support System: On your financial journey, you'll face challenges. A group can offer support, advice, and sometimes, just a listening ear.
- Collaborative Growth: Share resources, tips, and tools. Sometimes, another member might introduce you to a game-changing app or strategy.

Getting the Most from Groups:

- **Be Active:** Like any community, you get what you give. Engage, share, and support.
- **Stay Respectful:** Every member is on their unique journey. Respect differing opinions and experiences.
- **Safety First:** Especially in online groups, ensure you don't share sensitive personal or financial information.

5. Seek Mentors

Remember the wise old owl from storybooks, always offering sage advice? In the realm of finance, mentors play that crucial role.

The Value of a Mentor:

- **Personalized Guidance:** Unlike books or blogs, mentors can offer advice tailored specifically to your situation.
- **Avoid Pitfalls:** Benefit from their experience, avoiding mistakes they might have made.
- **Accountability:** Regular check-ins with a mentor can keep you on track.

Finding and Working with a Mentor:

- Identify a Good Fit: Not every expert will be the right mentor for you. Find someone whose expertise aligns with your goals.
- Mutual Respect: A mentor-mentee relationship is built on trust and respect.
- Reciprocity: While the mentor imparts wisdom, remember to give back. Even a fresh perspective (yours!) can be valuable to them.

Using imagery of the journey through this vast and dynamic forest for this chapter was to simply illustrate the realm of personal finance is just as vast and dynamic as you can imaging, even more so with the random anomalies the real world itself can throw your way. With changing economies, evolving market trends, and ever-shifting personal circumstances, the learning never truly stops. Embrace this continuous journey of education, and as you navigate the forest of finance, may your path always be lit by the torch of knowledge.

Chapter 10: Avoid Unnecessary Fees

Ten chapters in is coming a long way in mastering the art of personal finance management. But there's one villain with a sneaky way of chipping away at your hard-earned savings: unnecessary fees. These little culprits can add up over time and have a more significant impact than you might think. So, let's gear up and tackle them head-on.

1. Understand Bank Charges

Banks, as much as they're here to serve us, are businesses. And they have ways of making money off even the most cautious of us. Let's understand these charges better.

Common Bank Fees:

- Overdraft fees: This is charged when you spend more than you have in your account.
- Monthly maintenance fees: Some banks charge this for the pleasure of holding your money.

- ATM fees: Using an ATM that isn't in your bank's network can lead to extra charges.
- Foreign transaction fees: Traveling or shopping internationally? You might get hit with this one.

Combatting These Charges:

- Always be aware of your balance to avoid overdrafts.
- Use only in-network ATMs or consider banks that reimburse ATM fees.
- For avid travelers or international shoppers, look into bank cards that don't charge foreign transaction fees.
- If you're being charged monthly fees, it might be time to shop around for a bank that offers free checking accounts.

2. Pay Bills On Time

It sounds simple, doesn't it? Yet, with the hustle and bustle of life, it's easier than you might think to forget a due date.

The Impact:

- Late fees: These can add up, especially if you miss multiple bills.
- Interest: On some bills, like credit cards, missing a payment can mean accruing interest.
- Credit Score: Your payment history plays a significant role in your credit score. Late payments can lead to drops in this crucial number.

Keeping Up:

- Set up automatic payments, especially for recurring monthly bills.
- Use calendar reminders or dedicated apps that notify you about upcoming due dates.
- If you do forget, reach out to the service provider. Sometimes, they might waive the fee, especially if it's a rare oversight on your part.

3. Review Subscription Services

Subscription services are like the silent, almost invisible, ninjas of the financial world. They might seem small, but can they add up to massive amounts of your cash gone with little to show for it.

The Sneaky Truth:

- Many of us sign up for trials and then forget about them. Before you know it, you've been charged for a year of a service you barely use.
- Some services increase their fees over time.

Taking Control:

- Take an afternoon off and go through your bank statements. Highlight any recurring charges.
- Evaluate each service. Do you still use it? Is it providing value?
- Remember to cancel subscriptions that you don't need. For the ones you're keeping, check if there are any discounts or loyalty rewards available.

4. Be Wary of Investment Fees

Investing is an essential part of building wealth. But it's not just about the returns; it's also about the costs.

Common Investment Fees:

- Fund expense ratios: This is the cost of managing the fund, often associated with mutual funds or ETFs.
- Transaction fees: These are charged every time you buy or sell an investment.
- Advisory fees: If you have a financial advisor, they might charge this for managing your investments.

Reducing These Costs:

- Before investing in any fund, look at its expense ratio. Lower is usually better.
- Consider platforms that offer zero or minimal transaction fees.
- If you have an advisor, understand their fee structure. Some might charge a flat fee instead of a percentage, which might be more cost-effective as your investments grow.

5. Negotiate

You have more power than you think! Many fees and rates are negotiable. You have to be bold enough to ask.

Areas to Flex Your Negotiation Muscles:

- Credit card interest rates: Especially if you've been a long-time loyal customer.
- Bank fees: If you're slapped with an unexpected fee, it doesn't hurt to call and ask for it to be waived.
- Subscription services: Some might offer you a discount if you mention considering cancelation.

Perfecting the Art:

- Be polite but firm. Remember, the customer service representative is just doing their job.
- Do your homework. If you're asking for a lower credit card interest rate, know what other banks are offering.
- If one representative isn't helpful, consider calling back at a different time or speaking to someone higher up.

We are moving swiftly through this book and doing well as you continue your financial freedom journey. Stay alert, and keep an eye out for all those pesky fees. Just like you wouldn't let loose change fall through the holes in your pocket, ensure that unnecessary fees aren't creating holes in your financial plan. By staying vigilant and proactive, you can keep more of your money where it belongs – with you!

Chapter 11: Practice Regular Financial Reviews

Navigating through your personal finance data to maintain goals only works if you implement this simple habit of stability: regular financial reviews. Returning to the sailing metaphor, this is akin to a sea captain setting sail without periodically checking his compass or map. The ship is guaranteed to end up way off course. Similarly, by taking the time to assess your financial health routinely, you ensure your ship stays on the right track. Let's examine the crucial aspects of what a regular financial review can do for you.

1. Check Monthly Statements

When driving your car, you must constantly monitor your car's current speed and fuel reserves to ensure you reach your final destination with little incident. It would help you manage your money if you kept a close eye on your monthly financial statements with the same zest. This is your frontline defense against discrepancies, unexpected fees, and even fraud.

Why It's Vital:

- It keeps you aware of your spending habits.
- It alerts you to any unauthorized transactions.
- Monitoring statements can also remind you of recurring expenses, some of which you might no longer need.

Tips for Effective Checking:

- Set a specific date, say the first weekend of every month, as your "Statement Day."
- Use highlighters: green for planned expenses, yellow for unplanned but necessary, and red for what could be avoided.
- Consider financial management apps. They can categorize and visualize your expenses, making reviews easier.

2. Review Budget

Your budget is essentially your financial map. Regularly checking this map ensures you're still heading towards your desired destination.

The Importance of Budget Reviews:

- It ensures your budget is still relevant. Changes in income or expenses might necessitate budget adjustments.
- It allows you to measure your discipline and commitment.
- It's an opportunity to adjust and allocate for any unexpected expenses.

Steps to Effective Budget Reviews:

- Compare your actual spending against your budgeted amounts. How did you fare?
- Adjust categories if you consistently overspend or underspend in certain areas.
- Ensure you're not consistently using credit to bridge gaps in your budget. If you are, it's time for a change.

3. Evaluate Financial Goals

Goals give direction to your financial journey. But as life evolves, so might your goals. This step ensures you're still aligned with your aspirations.

Why Regular Goal Evaluation Matters:

- Personal circumstances change.
  Marriage, having kids, changing jobs, or
  sudden health concerns can all reshape
  your financial landscape.
- Re-evaluating keeps motivation high.
  Recognizing achievements boosts morale
  and commitment.

How to Review Effectively:

- Revisit the goals you set (short, medium,
  and long-term). Are they still relevant?
- Celebrate milestones, even the small
  ones!
- Adjust timelines if necessary. Be flexible,
  but always keep moving forward.

4. Assess Investments

If your financial journey is a voyage,
investments are the strong winds propelling
your ship forward. However, not all winds are
favorable, so a regular assessment is crucial.

Importance of Investment Assessments:

- The financial market is ever-changing. Today's winning stocks might be tomorrow's losers.
- Regular assessments can prevent potential major losses.
- It helps you recognize new opportunities.

Steps to Assessing Investments:

- Keep updated with market news. Knowledge is power.
- Consider the long-term trajectory. Short-term fluctuations are a part of the investment journey.
- Consult with financial advisors. Their expert perspective can be invaluable.

5. Rebalance Portfolio

Over time, due to market fluctuations, your investment portfolio might lean too heavily in one direction. Rebalancing ensures that your investments align with your desired risk tolerance.

Why Rebalancing is Essential:

- It maintains the desired level of risk. Without rebalancing, you might be exposed to more risk than you're comfortable with.
- It ensures diversification. Spreading investments reduces potential damage from any single sector's poor performance.

Effective Rebalancing Tips:

- Set a regular schedule, whether it's quarterly, bi-annually, or annually.
- Don't let emotions drive decisions. It's easy to become attached to specific stocks or sectors, but objectivity is key.
- Understand that rebalancing might sometimes mean selling high-performing assets to buy under-performers. It's all about maintaining the right balance.

Regular financial reviews serve as a compass that gives you the bearing of a true north for your personal finance journey. Recalibrations and recalculations will happen (reference your pesky GPS when you choose to take a 'wrong' turn after being given explicit instructions). It might seem tedious, even unnecessary, when financial times are running well, but when an unexpected storm of life hits—and they will—these regular checks ensure your financial health stays sound. You can maintain your current financial status, remain on course for your future goals, and possibly find a way to prosper from the chaos.

Chapter 12: Ensure Proper Insurance

When it comes to personal finance, many focus on savings, investments, and budgeting. But there's another critical element to consider: insurance. Think of insurance as your financial safety net. Having the right insurance coverage is not about expecting the worst but being prepared for it. Just as you wouldn't set sail without enough life preservers for all your passengers, you shouldn't attempt to navigate the waters of life without the right insurance coverage.

How do you ensure your personal safety net is robust, reliable, and tailored to all your needs? Let's delve deeper into the art of ensuring proper insurance.

1. Understand Needs

Before blindly jumping into the world of insurance policies, it's crucial to understand your unique needs. What works for your friend or neighbor might not be the best fit for you.

Factors to Consider:

- Life stage: A young, single professional will have different insurance needs than a parent with three children.
- Assets: From homes to cars to personal belongings, consider what you own and its value.
- Health: Your health condition and history can determine what type of medical insurance you should consider.
- Financial Dependents: Do you have family members relying on your income?

Steps to Understand Your Needs:

- Conduct a personal audit. List down your assets, dependents, and any other factors that might require insurance.
- Consider future needs. Are you planning to buy a house soon? Start a family? Your future plans will affect your insurance requirements.

2. Shop Around

With a clearer picture of your personal insurance needs, now is the time to go shopping! While this may not be as fun as window shopping for a stylish new outfit, it's undeniably more critical to take claim of proper insurance coverage.

Why Shopping Around is Essential:

- Variety: There are numerous insurance providers, each offering various policies with different terms and conditions.
- Cost: Premiums can vary significantly between providers. Shopping around ensures you get value for your money.
- Coverage: Not all policies are made equal. By exploring different options, you can find one that covers your specific needs comprehensively.

Effective Shopping Tips:

- Use comparison websites. They can provide a quick overview of the market offerings.
- Don't be shy to negotiate. Some agents might offer you better deals if they know you're considering multiple options.
- Read reviews. What are other customers saying about a particular insurance provider?

3. Re-evaluate Annually

Settling on an insurance policy isn't the end. As life evolves, so do your insurance needs.

Why Annual Re-evaluation is Crucial:

- Life changes: Significant life events, such as marriage, having children, or purchasing a new property, can change your insurance needs.
- Market shifts: Insurance providers regularly update their policies and offerings.
- Savings opportunity: You might find more competitive rates or better coverage options each year.

Conducting an Annual Review:

- Set a reminder. Choose a specific time of the year, like your birthday or the start of the year, to conduct your insurance review.
- Consult with professionals. An insurance agent can provide insights into new offerings that might be beneficial for you.

4. Avoid Being Over-insured

Having insurance is essential, but there's a thing as too much of a good thing. Over-insuring means you're paying for coverage you don't need.

Spotting Over-insurance:

- If your policy covers an amount that's significantly more than the value of an asset, you might be over-insured.
- If you have multiple policies that overlap, you're paying extra for the same coverage.

Preventing Over-insurance:

- Understand your policies. Regularly review the details to ensure you're only covered for what's necessary.
- Consult experts. They can provide guidance on the right amount of coverage for your assets and situation.

5. Understand the Details

Insurance policies can be a maze of jargon and fine print. But understanding these details is crucial to ensuring you have the right coverage.

Why Details Matter:

- They determine what is covered and what isn't. This is crucial information in case of a claim.
- They dictate the terms of the insurance contract, including premiums, payouts, and more.

Deciphering the Details:

- Ask for clarification. If there's anything you don't understand in the policy, ask your insurance provider or agent to explain.
- Consider legal advice. For significant policies, such as life insurance or property insurance, it might be worth having a legal professional review the terms.

You can not think of insurance as just another box to tick in your personal finance checklist. It's your financial lifeline, ensuring unexpected events don't derail your financial journey. By understanding your needs, shopping wisely, regularly re-evaluating, avoiding over-insurance, and grasping the policy details, you can rest easy knowing that, come what may, you do not lose your entire financial footing in the face of any devastating event.

Chapter 13: Plan for Taxes

Taxes – the inevitable and oft-dreaded part of any individual's financial journey. But let's put the grumbling aside for a moment and have a frank chat. Did you know that proper planning can transform taxes from a burdensome obstacle into a navigable part of your financial roadmap? Sounds intriguing? Let's see if we can adjust your views on personal taxes.

1. Understand Tax Brackets

What is a Tax Bracket Anyway?
A tax bracket represents the rate at which your income is taxed. As you earn more, you might move into a higher tax bracket, but only the income that falls within that bracket gets taxed at the higher rate.

The Basics:

- Progressive System: Many tax systems, like the U.S., are progressive. This means the more you earn, the higher percentage you pay, but only on the income in that higher bracket.

- Regular Updates: Tax laws and brackets often get revised based on legislation. Stay informed!
- State and Local Taxes: Depending on where you live, there might be additional state or local taxes to consider.

Takeaway:
By understanding which bracket you're in, you can make informed decisions. For instance, if a raise would push you into a higher bracket, but only slightly, the additional earnings might still be worth it after tax.

2. Leverage Tax-Advantaged Accounts

Remember those special accounts where your money gets VIP treatment from taxes? Those are tax-advantaged accounts, and they're like VIP lounges for your hard-earned cash.

Examples Include:

- 401(k) and IRAs: Retirement accounts where you can either contribute pre-tax dollars or enjoy tax-free withdrawals.
- HSAs (Health Savings Accounts): These allow you to save pre-tax dollars for qualified medical expenses.

- 529 Plans: Designed for education savings, with tax-free growth and withdrawals for qualified expenses.

Takeaway:
By strategically placing your money in these accounts, you can enjoy significant tax savings. It's like finding a legal shortcut in the tax maze!

3. Keep Good Records

There is an art to keeping financial records that goes beyond just scribbling in numbers in columns for your bookkeepers. Think of it as keeping a diary but for your finances. And during tax season, your past you will thank present you for being so diligent with your financial diary entries.

Why It's Essential:

- Proof of Expenses: If you're claiming deductions or credits, having receipts or records is crucial.
- Avoiding Over or Underpayment: Accurate records ensure you pay just the right amount, not a penny more or less.
- Peace of Mind: In the rare case of an audit, having organized records can make the process much smoother.

Takeaway:
Whether it's a digital tool, an app, or good old-fashioned folders and binders, find a system that works for you and stick to it. Consistency is key.

4. Consult with a Tax Professional

While DIY is admirable (and sometimes fun if you're into that sort of thing), taxes might be an area where you want an expert by your side.

Benefits of a Tax Pro:

- Stay Updated: Tax laws are like the weather in some places – constantly changing. Professionals keep up so you don't have to.
- Maximize Deductions: They can spot those often-overlooked deductions that can save you money.
- Minimize Mistakes: A simple error can lead to penalties. Having a pro can greatly reduce this risk.

Takeaway:
Consider it an investment, not an expense. The savings, both in money and peace of mind, can often outweigh the cost.

5. Plan Ahead

Remember the saying, "Failing to plan is planning to fail?" When it comes to taxes, truer words were never spoken.

Tips for Planning:

- Estimate Your Tax Bill: Based on your income, deductions, and credits, you can get an idea of what's coming.
- Adjust Withholdings: If you consistently owe a lot or get a huge refund, adjust your withholdings with your employer.
- Set Aside Self-Employment Taxes: Freelancers, listen up! Put away a portion of your earnings for taxes, so you're not caught off-guard.

Takeaway:
With taxes, the early bird doesn't just get the worm; it gets savings, peace of mind, and a stress-free tax season.

This book's final chapter completes your trip through 13 tips for financial success. With the conclusion of this chapter, I hope you are converted to the side of 'taxes are a misguided anti-hero' or to understand that they are not as much of a vile enemy as they are often portrayed. Think of taxes as a river. With the proper preparation, you can sail smoothly. Without it, you might find yourself paddling upstream. Understand those brackets, leverage special accounts, keep impeccable records, seek expert advice, and always plan ahead. After all, in the vast game of financial management, why let taxes be the wildcard when you can hold all the aces?

Conclusion: You Are Now (Mostly) A Master

So, you think you're a master of personal finances now?

Technically, yes. This book allows you access to an extensive trove of knowledge that, if you apply it, will contribute to the sustained health of your financial life. By reaching the end of this book, you've embarked on a journey of learning, strategizing, and decision-making to put your finances on the right track.

But a master? Let's use the following few pages to review what we've covered in your education on mastering personal finances.

Chapter 1: Set Clear Financial Goals

Remember the excitement you felt when you first set your financial goals? Whether buying a home, traveling the world, or simply achieving peace of mind, setting clear and achievable targets is the foundation for financial success. It's like plotting a destination in your GPS. You have won half the battle when you know where you want to go.

Chapter 2: Create a Budget

Once you set your goals, the next step is to map out how to get there. That's where budgeting comes into play. By allocating every dollar (or whatever your currency may be) a role, you take control of your finances rather than letting them control you. So keep that ledger close and continue tracking those expenses.

Chapter 3: Build an Emergency Fund

Life has a funny way of throwing curveballs at us. An emergency fund is like an umbrella for that unexpected financial rainstorm. Ideally, you'd want three to six months' worth of expenses stashed away, offering you a security blanket when you need it most.

Chapter 4: Reduce Debt

Debt can be a chain around your ankle, impeding your ability to advance in your financial journey. Reducing it, primarily the high-interest debts, frees up money for other endeavors and offers an incredible emotional and psychological lift. So, keep chipping away at it. Remember, every bit counts.

Chapter 5: Save Consistently

Just as a river is made drop by drop, your financial success will be built penny by penny. Make saving a consistent habit, no matter how small the amount. Over time, thanks to the magic of compound interest, those small savings can lead to significant gains.

Chapter 6: Invest Wisely

Speaking of gains, investing is a powerful way to grow your wealth. By understanding the basics of the stock market, bonds, and other investment vehicles and combining that knowledge with a dash of patience, you can watch your money work for you. Just remember the golden rule: Never invest money you can't afford to lose.

Chapter 7: Monitor Your Credit Score

Your credit score is like your financial report card. It is not the fabled 'permanent record' you were warned of in grade school, but it is one grade you want to maintain as close to A+ as possible. A good credit score can open doors to better interest rates, saving you money in the long run. Regularly monitoring it ensures you're on top of things and can address any discrepancies that might pop up.

Chapter 8: Live Below Your Means

This might sound a tad old-fashioned, but it's timeless and (financially) valuable advice. Living below your means isn't about denying yourself pleasures but enjoying life without the constant stress of debt. By spending less than you earn, you build a buffer that allows you to tackle opportunities or challenges head-on.

Chapter 9: Continuously Educate Yourself

The financial world is ever-evolving. By keeping yourself updated with the latest trends, news, and innovations, you position yourself for success. So, be it a workshop, an online course, or even this very book, always continue learning.

Chapter 10: Avoid Unnecessary Fees

Those pesky fees - they can add up before you know it! Always be on the lookout for hidden charges or fees in your financial dealings. This includes bank fees, service charges, and even late fees. By being vigilant, you save money that can be better used elsewhere.

Chapter 11: Practice Regular Financial Reviews

Just like you'd go for regular health check-ups, your finances need periodic reviews, too.

Whether monthly, quarterly, or yearly, take stock of where you stand, re-evaluate your goals, and adjust course if needed. It keeps you on track and helps identify potential problems early on.

Chapter 12: Ensure Proper Insurance

Insurance isn't just a necessary evil – it's a lifesaver when calamities strike. From health to home to auto, having the right insurance policies and coverage can mean the difference between a minor setback and a catastrophic loss.

Chapter 13: Plan for Taxes

Benjamin Franklin once said, "In this world, nothing can be said to be certain, except death and taxes." Planning for taxes can help you maximize deductions, reduce your taxable income, and ensure you don't get any nasty surprises during tax season.

We made quite the journey in this book, haven't we? Personal finance might sometimes seem overwhelming, but remember, every expert was once a beginner. By applying the principles from each chapter, consistently making wise choices, and staying informed, you're well on your way to becoming a master of your finances. You may not be a definitive 'master,' but your mastery will grow as you implement the ideas in this book, then pick up a few other books on personal finance, add more tips, and continue.

So, here's to a future of financial freedom and endless possibilities!

About The Author

J Cleveland Payne is a multifaceted individual whose accomplishments span across varied domains. A proud veteran, he served as an Officer in the U.S. Air Force, dedicating his years to the nation's service. His commitment to excellence extends to his impressive 25+ year radio and television broadcasting tenure, where he has left an indelible mark.

As an author, Payne's oeuvre is extensive, with multiple books to his credit, each reflecting his deep understanding of the subjects he chooses to explore. His entrepreneurial spirit shines through in his management of two burgeoning businesses, Fast Forward Business Properties, LLC, and More Better Media, LLC, testaments to his knack for business acumen and vision.

The academic world knows him as an adjunct professor at Shorter College, a distinguished Historically Black College and University (HBCU) in North Little Rock, Arkansas. His role there showcases his expertise and commitment to giving back to the community and shaping the next generation.

J Cleveland Payne's journey is also profoundly enriched by his role as a life-long student of leadership. His insights into leadership paradigms are sought after, and he has channeled this passion by coaching many in their personal and professional development. Since 2006, Payne has embraced the world of podcasting, further cementing his place as a significant voice in media and communication.

Above all, his diverse experiences and unending quest for knowledge make J Cleveland Payne an authoritative figure in many areas, a testament to a life dedicated to excellence, growth, and service.

Acknowledgments

This book is a slight shift from my typical style of writing. With that, I want to thank everyone who asked me the question in some shape or fashion, 'Well, why can't you do that thing?' It was the push to do this thing right here.

Thank you for sticking it out to the end and trusting me to teach a subject I'm not known for. Good luck, and hopefully, my lessons on getting your financial house in order will clear a hurdle for you to achieve more of your dream goals.

www.ingramcontent.com/pod-product-compliance
Lightning Source LLC
Chambersburg PA
CBHW062314290526
45794CB00005B/1797